Elevate Your Life:

Master the Power of The High 5 Habit

By

Susie T. Straka

Elevate Your Life

Copyright © 2023 by Susie T. Straka

All rights reserved. No part of this book may be duplicated, stored in a retrieval system, or transmitted in any form or by any means, electronic, mechanical, photocopying, soundtrack, or otherwise, without written permission from the author.

The information contained in this book is for all-purpose information purposes only. The author makes no representations or warranties of any kind, express or implied, about the completeness, accuracy, reliability, suitability, or availability of the information contained in this book. Any confidence you place in such material is therefore strictly at your own risk.

Elevate Your Life

TABLE OF CONTENTS

Elevate Your Life: 1
Introduction 4
Chapter 1 6
Understanding the High 5 Habit 6
Chapter 2 14
The 5 Habits of The High 5 Habit 14
Chapter 3 23
Building the Foundation for The High 5 Habit 23
Chapter 4 33
Implementing the High 5 Habits in Your Daily Life ..33
Chapter 5 44
Overcoming Challenges and Staying Motivated 44
Conclusion 55
Reflection on The High 5 Habit 55
Final Thoughts and Encouragement 61

Introduction

Elevate Your Life: Master the Power of The High 5 Habit is a comprehensive guide to transforming your life and reaching new heights of success, happiness, and fulfillment. This book offers a unique approach to personal development, drawing on the latest research in psychology, neuroscience, and behavioral science to provide a step-by-step blueprint for creating the five essential habits that will help you achieve your goals and dreams.

At the core of this book is the idea that small changes can make a big impact. By focusing on five key habits, you can build the foundation for a more fulfilling life and take control of your growth journey. The author, a seasoned expert in personal development, has distilled decades of experience and research into this powerful and practical guide, giving you the tools, you need to succeed.

Throughout the book, you will learn about the five key habits that form the cornerstone of this transformative program.

You'll discover how to develop the habit of mindfulness, which will help you cultivate a deeper awareness of the present moment and improve your emotional intelligence. You'll also learn how to create a habit of physical activity, which will give you the energy and motivation to tackle your daily tasks and challenges with confidence.

In addition to mindfulness and physical activity, you'll explore the power of positive relationships, the importance of personal growth, and the benefits of giving back to others. Each of these habits is essential for elevating your life, and the author provides detailed guidance on how to cultivate each one, from setting goals and tracking progress to overcoming obstacles and maintaining momentum.

Whether you're looking to improve your health, build meaningful relationships, achieve your professional goals, or simply live a more fulfilling life,

Elevate Your Life: Master the Power of The High 5 Habit has something for you. With its straightforward, practical approach and inspiring stories from people who have transformed their lives using these habits, this book is your blueprint for personal growth and success.

Chapter 1
Understanding the High 5 Habit

The High 5 Habit is a mindset that prioritizes five key aspects of life, which are health, relationships, finances, personal growth, and fun. It is a holistic approach to living that recognizes the interdependence of these areas and the importance of balancing them to achieve overall well-being. By focusing on the High 5, individuals can improve their quality of life and cultivate a sense of fulfillment and purpose.

Health

Health is the foundation of the High 5 Habit. It includes both physical and mental health and encompasses practices such as exercise, proper nutrition, stress management, and sleep. Good health is essential for all aspects of life, and by prioritizing it, individuals can increase their energy levels, reduce their risk of illness, and improve their overall well-being.

Relationships

Relationships are a key part of the High 5 Habit because they provide support, love, and connection. Strong relationships can help individuals feel valued and fulfilled and can provide a sense of community and belonging. To prioritize relationships, individuals should make time for loved ones, communicate openly, and actively listen and engage with others.

Finances

Finances are also a crucial part of the High 5 Habit. Financial stability allows individuals to meet their basic needs and provides a sense of security. It also provides the resources to pursue other aspects of the High 5, such as personal growth and fun. To prioritize finances, individuals should develop a budget, reduce debt, and save for the future.

Personal Growth

Personal growth is an ongoing procedure of self-improvement and self-discovery.

It involves setting and working towards personal goals, learning new skills, and taking on new challenges. Personal growth is an essential part of the High 5 Habit as it helps individuals develop a sense of purpose, increase their self-esteem, and deepen their sense of fulfillment.

Fun

Finally, the High 5 Habit includes fun. Life is not all about work and responsibility, and it is important to make time for leisure activities that bring joy and happiness. Fun activities can help reduce stress, boost mood, and improve overall well-being. To prioritize fun, individuals should engage in activities that bring them joy and spend time with loved ones.

In conclusion, the High 5 Habit is a holistic approach to living that prioritizes five key aspects of life: health, relationships, finances, personal growth, and fun. By balancing these areas, individuals can achieve overall well-being and cultivate a sense of fulfillment and purpose.

The High 5 Habit encourages individuals to take an active role in their lives and to make conscious choices that support their health and happiness.

The Importance of Incorporating the High 5 Habits in Your Life

The High 5 Habits are habits that have been proven to help individuals live healthier and more successful life. They are: Eat Well, Train Hard, Rest Smart, Play Hard and Love Hard. Incorporating these habits into one's life can be incredibly beneficial, as they are habits that are proven to help people reach their goals and increase their overall quality of life.

Eating well is essential to maintaining good health and can help people achieve a healthy weight, prevent disease, and improve overall well-being. Eating a variety of nutritious foods, avoiding processed and unhealthy foods, and maintaining portion control is essential for good health. Eating well can also help to reduce stress, provide energy, and improve mood.

Training hard is another important habit that can help individuals reach their goals. With regular exercise, individuals can improve their physical health and strengthen their bodies. Exercise also helps to decrease stress and improve mental health. Additionally, regular exercise can help to reduce the risk of many diseases and can even help to improve cognitive function.

Resting smart is an important part of maintaining good health. Getting enough sleep is essential for proper functioning and can help to reduce stress, improve concentration, and keep the body healthy. Additionally, taking breaks throughout the day can help to clear the mind and recharge the body.

Playing hard is a great way to have fun and can help to reduce stress, improve relationships, and increase happiness. Taking time to have fun, be creative, and spend time with loved ones is essential for overall well-being.

Finally, loving hard is a habit that is essential for good health. Taking time to be kind, patient, and understanding with oneself and others is essential for maintaining good relationships and mental health.

Additionally, showing appreciation and love to those around us can help to improve our overall quality of life.

Incorporating the High 5 Habits into one's life can be incredibly beneficial, as they are proven to help individuals reach their goals and lead healthier and more successful life. Taking the time to eat well, train hard, rest smart, play hard, and love hard can help individuals to improve their physical and mental health, reduce stress, and increase their happiness and overall quality of life.

Benefits of The High 5 Habit

The High 5 Habit is a simple yet powerful habit that can help improve the quality of life for individuals and teams. It involves giving out five high fives at the end of each day to recognize, appreciate, and celebrate successes, successes that may be small or large.

The High 5 Habit is beneficial for numerous reasons. First, it's an incredibly easy way to show appreciation for someone's efforts, no matter how small.

Giving a high five can be a simple, yet meaningful gesture that can make someone's day. It can also be an effective way to build relationships between coworkers, as it creates an opportunity to bond with one another and celebrate each other's successes.

Second, the High 5 Habit can help boost motivation and morale. Receiving recognition for one's efforts can be a great motivator and can help people feel more valued and appreciated. This can lead to increased productivity as people are more motivated to work harder and strive for better results.

Third, it can create a team mentality. By recognizing each other's successes, team members can be reminded that they are all working towards a common goal which can help to boost morale and motivation.

Fourth, the High 5 Habit can help to reinforce positive behavior. By recognizing and celebrating successes, people are more likely to repeat those positive behaviors in the future. This can help to build trust, collaboration, and respect between team members.

Finally, the High 5 Habit can be used to recognize larger achievements as well. While it is often used to recognize smaller successes, it can also be used to celebrate larger achievements such as promotions, awards, or other significant accomplishments. Doing this can help to build a stronger sense of pride and commitment to the team.

Overall, the High 5 Habit is a powerful way to show appreciation, build relationships, motivate people, and reinforce positive behaviors. It can be a simple yet meaningful way to recognize and celebrate successes, both big and small.

Chapter 2

The 5 Habits of The High 5 Habit

Habit 1: Physical Health

Physical health is an integral component of overall health and well-being and is defined as a state of being in which the body is functioning optimally, both physically and mentally. It is the result of engaging in activities that strengthen the body and enhance its physical condition, such as regular exercise, healthy eating, adequate sleep, and stress management. Physical health is also affected by a person's environment, including access to healthcare, nutritious food, and safe places to exercise.

Physical health is important because it contributes to an individual's overall well-being and quality of life. Regular physical activity helps reduce the risk of developing chronic health conditions such as heart disease, type 2 diabetes, and some cancers. It also helps to manage stress, boost mood and energy levels, improve sleep, and strengthen the immune system.

Physical health is achieved through a combination of diet, exercise, and lifestyle changes. Eating a healthy, balanced diet is essential for physical health, as it provides the body with the nutrients it needs to function properly. Exercise is also essential for physical health, as it helps to maintain muscle strength, improve cardiovascular health, and reduce the risk of chronic diseases. Additionally, lifestyle changes, such as quitting smoking and drinking alcohol in moderation, can help improve physical health.

In conclusion, physical health is a crucial component of overall health and well-being and is achieved through a combination of healthy eating, regular exercise, and lifestyle changes. By taking steps to improve physical health, individuals can enjoy a higher quality of life and reduce their risk of developing chronic health conditions.

Habit 2: Mental Health

Mental health is a state of emotional and psychological well-being where an individual can successfully cope with the everyday stresses of life, work effectively and make meaningful contributions to their community. Mental health is fundamental to an individual's overall health and well-being and is affected by the individual's physical health, lifestyle, attitudes, relationships, experiences, thoughts, and emotions.

Mental health is characterized by a variety of symptoms, including positive emotions such as happiness, joy, and self-confidence, as well as negative emotions such as depression, anxiety, and stress. Mental health is also affected by an individual's access to resources such as healthcare, education, employment, and social support, as well as their environment.

Mental health problems can range from mild to severe and can include anxiety, depression, bipolar disorder, schizophrenia, eating disorders, and other forms of mental illness. Mental health conditions can have a significant impact on an individual's life and can affect their ability to perform everyday activities, interact with others, and manage their emotions.

Achieving and maintaining good mental health is essential to overall health and well-being.

Mental health can be improved through a variety of methods including lifestyle changes, such as getting more exercise, eating healthier, and managing stress. Additionally, engaging in activities that promote personal growth, such as cognitive-behavioral therapy, can be beneficial in improving mental health and reducing symptoms of mental illness. It is important to seek help from a mental health professional if symptoms worsen or persist, as early intervention can be very beneficial in managing mental health issues.

Habit 3: Emotional Health

Emotional health is a state of well-being in which an individual can cope with the normal stresses of life, work productively, and make meaningful contributions to his or her community. It is about feeling good about one's self and having the ability to manage one's thoughts and feelings. Emotional health is closely related to mental health, but it goes beyond just managing mental health issues. It involves cultivating positive emotions, such as joy, contentment, and satisfaction, and maintaining a healthy balance between positive and negative emotions.

Elevate Your Life

To maintain emotional health, it is important to understand and manage one's feelings, thoughts, and behaviors. This involves learning to recognize and healthily express emotions, developing effective problem-solving skills, developing positive relationships and communication skills, and engaging in self-care activities. It also involves being aware of one's triggers and learning coping strategies to manage difficult emotions.

It is important to recognize that emotional health is closely connected to physical health. Developing healthy lifestyle habits, such as eating a balanced diet, getting enough sleep, and exercising regularly, can help maintain emotional health. Additionally, it is important to pay attention to any warning signs of mental health issues, such as feelings of helplessness, difficulty concentrating, and persistent feelings of sadness or anger. If these symptoms persist, it is important to reach out for professional help.

Emotional health is essential for overall well-being. Taking care of one's emotional health can help reduce stress, improve relationships, and promote a sense of purpose and fulfillment in life.

It is important to remember that emotional health is not static, but rather something that can be cultivated and improved upon over time.

Habit 4: Financial Health

Financial health is the state of one's finances, which can include anything from budgeting and saving to investing and planning for retirement. It is the ability to manage your money responsibly and effectively so that you can reach your goals and live a financially secure life. Financial health is important because it helps you make sound decisions about your money, which can have a positive impact on your overall well-being.

Achieving financial health involves understanding your current financial situation, setting financial goals, and creating a plan to reach those goals. To get started, it's important to track your income and expenses to get a clear picture of where your money is going. This will help you create a budget that works for you and your life. Once you have a budget, you can start to set realistic financial goals and create a plan to reach them.

This could involve cutting back on expenses, increasing your income, or both.

When it comes to investing, financial health also involves understanding the different types of investments and the risks associated with them. It's important to understand the potential return on your investments and the timeframe in which you may expect to see those returns. Additionally, it's important to diversify your investments to reduce risk.

It's also important to plan for the future, including retirement. This means understanding different types of retirement accounts, such as IRAs, 401(k)s, and Roth IRAs, and how to use them to save for retirement. Additionally, it's important to consider how taxes and inflation will affect your savings and investments over time.

Finally, it's important to be aware of the potential risks associated with financial products and services, as well as potential scams to avoid. It's also important to protect yourself from identity theft by using strong passwords, avoiding suspicious emails and websites, and regularly monitoring your accounts.

Financial health is an ongoing process that takes commitment and dedication. It's important to regularly review and adjust your financial plan to make sure it's on track and that you're making progress toward your goals. Additionally, seeking professional advice can be beneficial to ensure that you're making the best decisions for your financial future.

Habit 5: Spiritual Health

Spiritual health is the ability to find meaning and purpose in life, to be able to maintain hope and optimism, to be able to have a sense of belonging and trust, and develop relationships. It is often linked to having a sense of belonging and connection to a higher power and/or a set of beliefs or values that give life meaning.

Spiritual health is not limited to religion, although many people find spiritual satisfaction and fulfillment through organized religion. It is also possible to experience a sense of spiritual connection, meaning, and purpose even if one does not have a religious affiliation.

Having a sense of spiritual health is associated with the ability to cope with stress, maintain positive relationships, have a sense of purpose, and be able to identify what is important in life and live accordingly. Those with spiritual health tend to have a greater appreciation for life and can foster healthy relationships and be more compassionate, understanding, and tolerant.

Spiritual health is important for overall well-being. It is linked to physical and mental health, as those with strong spiritual health tend to have lower rates of depression, anxiety, and other mental health difficulties, and are more likely to have improved eating and exercise habits.

Spiritual health can be developed through a variety of activities such as meditation, prayer, yoga, journaling, and reading. These activities can help to cultivate a sense of connection to something greater than oneself, foster a sense of purpose and meaning, and increase appreciation for life. Additionally, regular activities such as attending church, synagogue, temple, or mosque, can help to build spiritual health.

Chapter 3

Building the Foundation for The High 5 Habit

Building the Foundation for The High 5 Habit is a process that can help individuals, teams, and organizations develop the necessary behaviors and skills to be successful. It involves a series of steps that focus on creating the environment, setting expectations, reinforcing positive behaviors, and recognizing and rewarding performance.

The first step is to create an environment in which the desired behavior is encouraged and expected. This starts with clearly defining the expectations of the group or organization and communicating those expectations to all members. This includes setting goals and objectives, developing processes and procedures, providing resources and support, and creating a culture of trust.

The second step is to reinforce the desired behaviors. This can be done by providing recognition and rewards for those who exhibit the desired behavior. It is also important to provide feedback on areas of improvement.

The third step is to recognize and reward performance. This is done by providing meaningful and appropriate recognition when team members or individuals reach their goals or objectives. It is also important to have rewards that are tailored to the individual or team.

The fourth step is to continue to support and cultivate the desired behavior. This involves providing ongoing coaching and feedback, providing resources and tools, and continuing to recognize and reward performance.

The fifth and final step is to ensure that the desired behavior is maintained. This is done by creating a system of accountability and providing ongoing support and guidance. This includes ensuring that all members of the team or organization understand their roles and responsibilities and providing regular check-ins to ensure that everyone is on track.

Building the Foundation for The High 5 Habit is an important process for any team or organization to ensure success. By creating an environment of trust and providing clear expectations, reinforcing positive behaviors, and recognizing and rewarding performance, teams and organizations can build the foundation for The High 5 Habit and create an environment that supports the desired behaviors and skills.

Understanding Your Current Habits

Understanding your current habits is an important step in achieving your goals. It can help you identify behaviors that are getting in the way of success and give your insight into how to make better choices in the future.

The first step in understanding your current habits is to identify them. This involves taking a close look at your daily activities and behaviors. Make a list of all the activities and habits you engage in regularly. This could include things like what time you wake up each day, whether you exercise, how much time you spend on social media, or what you eat for breakfast.

Once you've identified your current habits, it's time to assess them. Ask yourself questions like: Does this habit help or hinder me from achieving my goals? Do I have enough time for this habit? Is this habit beneficial for my mental or physical health?

Once you've identified your current habits and assessed their impacts on your life, it's time to create a plan for changing them. This plan should include setting realistic goals, creating a timeline for reaching those goals, and developing strategies for staying on track.

For example, if you've identified that you spend too much time on social media, your plan could include limiting the time you spend on it each day, replacing it with more productive activities, and tracking your progress.

Finally, it's important to be patient and kind to yourself as you work to change your habits. Habits are hard to break and it takes time to create lasting change. Be sure to recognize and celebrate your successes, no matter how small, as you go.

Elevate Your Life

Understanding your current habits is an important step in achieving your goals and creating positive change in your life. Identifying, assessing, and creating a plan for changing them can help you make better choices and achieve success.

Evaluating Your Current Habits

Evaluating your current habits is an essential step in developing a successful lifestyle and achieving your goals. It is important to take the time to reflect on your habits, both good and bad, to make changes that will improve your health, happiness, and overall well-being.

The first step in evaluating your current habits is to reflect on your day-to-day activities. What do you spend your time doing? Are you eating healthy meals, getting enough exercise, and getting enough sleep? Are you engaging in activities that bring you joy and help you reach your goals? It is also important to think about the mental state you are in throughout the day. Are you feeling rushed and stressed, or are you relaxed and focused?

Elevate Your Life

The next step is to take a look at the bigger picture. What is your long-term plan? Are you working towards achieving your goals? Are you taking steps to improve your life? Are you devoting in yourself and your future? Are you surrounding yourself with positive people and environments?

Once you have evaluated your current habits, it is time to make changes. Identify which habits are beneficial and which need to be changed. Make a plan for how to implement the changes and stick to it. Set realistic goals, and reward yourself when you reach them.

Finally, be patient with yourself. Making changes takes time, and it is important to remember that you are in control of your life. Evaluating your current habits and making the necessary changes will help you reach your goals and lead a healthier, happier life.

Setting Goals and Objectives

Setting goals and objectives is the cornerstone of any successful business.

Goals and objectives provide direction, inspiration, and motivation for employees and are essential for achieving desired results.

Goals are broad statements of desired outcomes, typically focusing on the "big picture" for the organization. Goals are often long-term and can range from achieving organizational growth to improving customer service. Goals can be set for any level of the organization, from the individual to the team to the entire organization.

Objectives are more specific than goals and are typically shorter-term. Objectives are measurable and attainable and provide the roadmap needed to reach the desired goal. Objectives are the "how" of the goal, providing the details of what needs to be done to achieve the desired outcome.

When setting goals and objectives, there are a few key points to consider. First, the goals and objectives should be realistic and achievable. The goals should be challenging, yet achievable, and should provide achievable targets for employees. The objectives should provide detailed steps needed to reach the desired goal. Finally, the goals and objectives should be aligned with the overall objectives of the organization.

Goals and objectives should be regularly reviewed and revised as needed. This ensures that the goals and objectives are still relevant and achievable. The regular review also allows the organization to track progress and make any necessary changes along the way.

Setting goals and objectives are essential for any successful organization. Goals provide the direction and motivation needed to reach the desired results. Objectives provide the roadmap needed to reach those goals. When setting goals and objectives, it is important to ensure that they are realistic, achievable, and aligned with the overall objectives of the organization. Regularly reviewing and revising the goals and objectives is also important to ensure that they are still relevant and achievable.

Creating a Plan of Action

Creating a Plan of Action is an important step in any project or task. It is a way to help organize thoughts and plan for the steps needed to reach a goal. A Plan of Action is a type of action plan that outlines the objectives, goals, strategies, and resources that will be needed to accomplish a desired outcome.

The first step in creating Action plans is to identify the goal. It is important to have a clear and concise goal in mind before taking any action. This goal should be measurable and achievable. Once the goal is determined, it is important to determine what resources are available and what strategies can be used to reach the goal. This can include gathering data, researching, networking, and consulting with experts.

The next step is to break down the goal into smaller, achievable tasks. This can be done by creating a timeline and outlining the steps needed to complete the goal. This timeline should include specific dates, deadlines, and milestones. It is important to be realistic about the amount of time needed to complete each task.

Once the timeline and tasks are determined, it is important to identify the resources needed to complete the plan. This includes people, tools, finances, materials, and other resources. It is important to account for all of the resources needed and to ensure that they are available.

The final step in creating Action plans is to review the plan and make necessary changes. This includes evaluating the timeline and making sure it is realistic and achievable. It is also important to review the tasks and resources and make sure they are still necessary and available. Once the plan is complete, it is important to monitor and track progress to ensure the plan is being followed and goals are being met.

Creating a Plan of Action is an important step in any project or task. It is a way to help organize thoughts and plan for the steps needed to reach a goal. It is important to be realistic about the timeline and resources needed to complete the plan. It is also important to review the plan and make necessary changes to ensure the goal is achievable and the plan is being followed.

Chapter 4

Implementing the High 5 Habits in Your Daily Life

The High 5 Habit is a simple yet powerful practice that can help you become more mindful, productive, and successful in your everyday life. It is based on the idea that if you start small and build on your successes, you can create a strong foundation for achieving big goals.

Here are five steps to implementing the High 5 Habit into your daily life.

1. Set a Goal: Set a specific, measurable goal that you would like to achieve. This will be your main focus and will help you stay on track with your desired results.

2. Break It Down: Break down your goal into smaller, manageable pieces. This will make it easier to focus on one task at a time and create a plan for moving forward.

3. Take Action: Once you have broken down your goal into smaller tasks, it's time to take action. Start with small steps and work your way up.

4. Celebrate Your Successes: As you work towards achieving your goal, celebrate your successes along the way. This will help to motivate you to continue working towards your goal.

5. Reflect on Your Progress: Finally, take the time to reflect on your progress. This will help you to identify the areas where you need to focus more effort and make adjustments if needed.

By following these five steps, you can create a strong foundation for achieving your goals and become more mindful, productive, and successful in your everyday life. Implementing the High 5 Habit will help you stay focused, organized, and motivated to reach your goals.

Incorporating Physical Health

Incorporating physical health into your daily life can have numerous benefits.

Elevate Your Life

Physical health is vital for overall health and well-being. It is necessary for mental and emotional health, and can even help to reduce stress and improve sleep quality.

Physical activity helps to strengthen muscles and bones and increases energy levels. It also aids in weight loss and weight management, as well as increasing metabolism. Regular physical activity can also help to reduce the risk of many chronic diseases, such as heart disease, diabetes, and some types of cancer. Additionally, physical activity can help to reduce symptoms of depression, anxiety, and stress.

There are many different ways to incorporate physical health into your life. You can start by incorporating exercise into your daily routine. Aim to get at least 150 minutes of moderate-intensity aerobic activity or 75 minutes of vigorous-intensity aerobic activity each week, as well as two days of muscle-strengthening activities. You can also incorporate activities such as walking, jogging, cycling, swimming, skipping, or even dancing into your daily routine.

Elevate Your Life

In addition to regular exercise, it is also important to incorporate healthy habits into your lifestyle. Eating a balanced diet, getting enough sleep, and limiting the amount of time spent sitting are all important for physical health. It is also important to stay hydrated and maintain a healthy weight.

Finally, it is important to prioritize mental and emotional health as well. Taking time for yourself and engaging in activities that bring joy can help to reduce stress and improve overall well-being. Incorporating relaxation techniques such as yoga, meditation, or mindfulness can also help to reduce stress and increase feelings of calm.

Incorporating physical health into your life can have many positive benefits. With a little bit of dedication and planning, you can easily incorporate physical activity, healthy habits, and relaxation techniques into your daily routine and improve your overall mental and physical health.

Improving Mental Health

Improving mental health is an important goal for individuals, communities, and society as a whole. Mental health plays a vital role in our overall well-being, and taking steps to look after our mental health can help us to lead healthier, more fulfilling lives.

There are many different strategies for improving mental health, which can involve both physical and mental activity. For example, physical activity such as exercise helps to boost self-esteem, reduce stress and anxiety, and increase feelings of well-being. Similarly, mental activities such as mindfulness, cognitive behavioral therapy, and self-care activities can help to develop skills for managing difficult thoughts and feelings, and help to reduce stress and anxiety.

Good nutrition and sleep are also important for maintaining good mental health. Eating a balanced diet, avoiding unhealthy foods and drinks, and getting enough sleep are all important for helping to manage stress and anxiety, and improve overall mood.

Social support is also important for improving mental health. Connecting with friends and family, or joining a support group, can help to reduce feelings of isolation and loneliness, which are often triggers for poor mental health.

Finally, it is important to remember that mental health is not static, and it is important to recognize that mental health can fluctuate over time. Taking steps to improve mental health can help to build resilience and provide strategies for coping with difficult times. Professional help can also be beneficial in managing mental health, and it is important to seek help if needed.

Managing Emotional Health

Emotional health is an important part of overall health and well-being. It involves being aware of, understanding, and managing one's emotions. It's a skill that needs to be developed and practiced throughout life to maintain a healthy emotional balance.

Managing emotional health can involve a variety of strategies, such as developing good coping skills, engaging in self-care activities, and seeking help when needed.

Developing Good Coping Skills: Coping skills are techniques that can help people manage their emotional responses to stress and difficult situations. Examples of coping skills include deep breathing, mindfulness, problem-solving, and relaxation. Learning and practicing specific coping skills can help people better manage their emotional responses to stress and difficult situations.

Engaging in Self-Care Activities: Self-care refers to activities that people do to take care of their physical, mental, and emotional health. Examples of self-care activities include getting enough sleep, eating a healthy diet, exercising, avoiding drugs and alcohol, and spending time with friends and family. Engaging in self-care activities can help people stay emotionally healthy and better manage their emotions.

Seeking Help When Needed: Sometimes, it's necessary to seek help from a mental health professional to manage emotions effectively.

A therapist can provide support, guidance, and strategies to help people better manage their emotions. Additionally, if a person is experiencing depression, anxiety, or other mental health concerns, a therapist may be able to provide treatment.

In conclusion, emotional health is an important part of overall health and well-being. It involves being aware of, understanding, and managing one's emotions. To do this, people can develop good coping skills, engage in self-care activities, and seek help when needed.

Building Financial Health

Building financial health involves understanding the basics of personal finance and implementing steps to increase one's financial security. This includes managing spending, saving, investing, and protecting against financial risks.

The first step in building financial health is to create a budget. A budget is a plan for how to spend and save money.

It should include all income and expenses, including fixed costs (such as rent and utilities) and variable costs (such as groceries and entertainment). By creating a budget, you will be able to identify areas where you can save money and create a plan to pay off debts.

The next step is to start saving. It is important to save a portion of your income to help ensure financial security. This could be done through a savings account, retirement account, or other investment vehicles. The amount you save should be determined by your budget and goals.

The third step is to invest. Investing is the process of using money to purchase assets such as stocks, bonds, mutual funds, and real estate, with the hope of growing the value of the investment over time. Investing can be a great way to help build wealth and achieve financial goals.

The fourth step is to protect against financial risks. This includes having an emergency fund, insurance, and other financial products. An emergency deposit is a savings account that can be used to cover unexpected expenses.

Insurance can help protect against financial losses due to health care expenses, property damage, or other risks.

These four steps are the basics of building financial health. It is important to remember that building financial health is a process and it takes time. It is also important to seek professional advice if you have questions or need assistance.

Fostering Spiritual Health

Fostering spiritual health is an important part of overall health and well-being. It involves developing and nurturing a relationship with something greater than oneself, such as a higher power, nature, or a sense of connectedness. This can be done through regular spiritual practices such as prayer, meditation, yoga, and contemplation. Spiritual health is important because it can help to provide a sense of purpose, peace, and fulfillment. It can also provide a source of comfort and strength during difficult times.

Spiritual health involves developing a positive relationship with oneself and with the world around us. This includes cultivating self-awareness and understanding, as well as self-care and compassion. It also involves being mindful of our thoughts and feelings and recognizing the interconnectedness of all things. Additionally, spiritual health includes developing values and a sense of purpose in life.

One way to foster spiritual health is to engage in spiritual practices such as prayer, meditation, yoga, and contemplation. These practices can help to create a connection with something greater than ourselves, as well as provide a sense of relaxation and calm. Additionally, reading spiritual texts and engaging in spiritual activities, such as volunteering and service, can help to strengthen our spiritual health.

Finally, it is important to recognize that spiritual health is a personal journey and that it looks different for everyone. It is important to find what works for you and to keep exploring until you find something that resonates with you. Taking time to reflect and connect with yourself and the world around you can help to foster spiritual health.

Chapter 5

Overcoming Challenges and Staying Motivated

Overcoming challenges and staying motivated can be difficult, especially when we're faced with obstacles that seem insurmountable. It's easy to give up, but it's important to remember that every challenge is an opportunity to grow and learn.

The first step to overcoming challenges and staying motivated is to identify your goals. It's important to set realistic and achievable goals, as this will help you to stay on track. Make sure to break down large goals into smaller achievable steps to make them more manageable.

Once you have identified your goals, it's important to create a plan of action. This plan should include specific steps to take, a timeline, and potential resources to use. It's also important to give yourself time to plan and review your progress regularly.

It's also important to stay positive and focus on the progress you have made. Celebrating your successes, no matter how small, can help to motivate you to keep going. It's also important to keep in mind that there will likely be setbacks along the way, and not to get discouraged by them.

It's also helpful to create a support system. This could include friends, family, or even a mentor. Having a support system that can provide advice and encouragement can be invaluable when it comes to overcoming challenges and staying motivated.

Finally, it's vital to take care of yourself physically and mentally. Make sure to take regular breaks and get plenty of sleep to ensure that you're in the best possible position to tackle your challenges.

By following these steps and staying focused on your goals, you can overcome any challenge and stay motivated to keep going.

Common Challenges and Obstacles

Common challenges and obstacles are issues that arise in any organization or any situation. They can be caused by external factors such as the economy, competition, or changes in the environment, or they can be caused by internal factors such as organizational structure, staffing, or leadership. It is important to recognize and address common challenges and obstacles to create a successful and productive business environment.

The most common challenges and obstacles faced by organizations are:

1. Change Management: Change is a fact of life in organizations. Companies must be able to adapt to new trends, technologies, and regulations to remain competitive. Change management requires an understanding of how to create an environment that is conducive to change, as well as how to plan, implement, and manage change initiatives.

2. Leadership: Leadership is essential for an organization to succeed. Leaders need to be able to create and sustain a vision for the future, motivate and inspire employees, and provide direction and clarity.

They need to be able to manage and lead teams effectively and make decisions that are in the best interest of the organization.

3. Communication: Communication is key to any successful organization. It is important to ensure that information is regularly shared and that there is an effective communication network in place. It is also important to ensure that messages are clear, concise, and communicated on time.

4. Staffing and Talent Management: Having the right people in the right roles is essential for an organization to succeed. It is important to have an effective recruitment and selection process in place, as well as a comprehensive talent management system.

5. Organizational Culture: Establishing a strong organizational culture is key to any successful organization. It is important to create an environment where employees feel valued, respected, and motivated.

6. Technology: Technology is an integral part of any business today. Organizations need to stay up to date with the latest technologies to remain competitive.

They need to ensure that they have the right tools, processes, and systems in place to remain efficient and effective.

By recognizing and addressing common challenges and obstacles, organizations can create a successful and productive business environment. It is important to develop effective strategies and plans to overcome these issues to ensure success.

Staying Motivated and Committed

Staying motivated and committed is essential to achieving success in any endeavor. It is the internal drive that helps us push through difficult times and keeps us focused on achieving our goals. To stay motivated and committed, it is important to create a plan of action and set realistic and achievable goals. It is also important to reward yourself for your successes and recognize your accomplishments.

Creating a plan of action can help you stay motivated and committed to reaching your goals.

Elevate Your Life

Break down your goals into smaller, achievable steps so that they seem more manageable. This will help you focus your efforts and stay on way.

Setting realistic goals is also important in staying motivated and committed. If your goals are too far out of reach, it can be difficult to stay focused on them. Set realistic goals that are attainable and that you can measure your progress against. Make sure to set goals that are challenging but reachable.

Rewarding yourself for success is a great way to keep motivation and commitment high. Celebrate your actions, no matter how small they may be. Acknowledge your progress and reward yourself for the hard work you've put in.

Finally, recognizing your accomplishments is key to staying motivated and committed. Reflect on your successes and take pride in your achievements. This will help keep you motivated and encourage you to continue striving for success.

Elevate Your Life

By creating a plan of action, setting realistic goals, rewarding yourself for successes, and recognizing your accomplishments, you can stay motivated and committed to achieving your goals. Staying motivated and committed is essential to achieving success, so make sure to take the time to focus on these important steps.

Celebrating Progress and Success

Celebrating progress and success is an important part of any successful business or organization, as it gives people the incentive and motivation to continue striving and pushing for better results. Celebrating progress and success is a way to recognize and reward individuals or teams for their hard work and accomplishments. When people feel appreciated and rewarded for their efforts, they are more likely to stay committed to the organization and continue working hard.

There are various ways to celebrate progress and success, such as employee recognition awards, team-building activities, and company-wide celebrations.

Recognizing individual and team successes is a great way to show appreciation and encourage people to continue working hard. Employee recognition awards can be given for achievements such as completing a project on time, exceeding expectations, or taking initiative on a task. Team-building activities can be a fun way to celebrate progress and success and can include anything from a team lunch, to a team-building retreat, or even a company-wide celebration.

Company-wide celebrations can be a great way to recognize and reward employees for their hard work and achievements. This type of celebration can include anything from a company picnic, to an awards ceremony, or even an all-expenses-paid trip. Celebrating progress and success is also a great way to build morale and create a positive work environment. When people feel appreciated and rewarded for their efforts, they are more likely to stay committed to the organization and continue working hard.

In conclusion, celebrating progress and success is an important part of any successful business or organization. It is a great way to recognize and reward individuals and teams for their hard work and accomplishments. There are various ways to celebrate progress and success, such as employee recognition awards, team-building activities, and company-wide celebrations. Celebrating progress and success can help to build morale and create a positive work environment, which is essential for any successful organization.

Maintaining The High 5 Habit for Life

Maintaining the High 5 habit for life is a commitment to making positive lifestyle changes and staying true to five core habits that will help you thrive both mentally and physically.

The five core habits are:

1. Move Your Body - Regular exercise is essential for mental and physical health, so make sure to get moving.

Elevate Your Life

Whether it's a daily walk, an intense workout, or just a few minutes of stretching, your body needs movement to stay healthy.

2. Nourish Your Body - Eating healthy, nutrient-dense foods is essential for optimal health. Make sure to comprise a variety of fruits, vegetables, whole grains, lean proteins, and healthy fats in your diet.

3. Connect with Others - Social connections are essential for our mental and emotional well-being. Make sure to take time to reconnect with friends and family, as well as make new connections.

4. Find Time for Yourself - It's important to make time for yourself, whether it's meditating, journaling, reading, or just taking a few moments to sit and be still.

5. Give Back - Giving back to your community is a great way to stay connected and feel fulfilled. Find ways to volunteer your time and talents to make a difference in the world.

Maintaining the High 5 habit for life requires dedication and commitment. It's important to be consistent and keep up with your habits daily.

Elevate Your Life

You may need to adjust your routine as life changes, but the key is to stay focused on your overall goal. Make sure to set realistic goals and celebrate your successes along the way. If you find yourself struggling, don't be afraid to ask for help or support. Lastly, remember to be kind to yourself and show yourself some grace.

Conclusion

Reflection on The High 5 Habit

Reflection on The High 5 Habit is a method of self-reflection that encourages individuals to reflect on their behavior and attitude by considering five specific habits that are essential for personal growth and development. ***The five habits are:***

1. Have a Positive Attitude: Having a positive attitude is essential for any successful endeavor. It is important to have a positive attitude even when things become difficult. This will help you to stay motivated and focused on the task at hand and will also help you to stay on track with your goals.

2. Set Goals: Setting goals is important to stay motivated and on track with your efforts. It is important to have both short and long-term goals to ensure that you are progressing in the right direction.

3. Work Hard: Working hard is essential to achieve your goals. It is important to put in the necessary effort to succeed.

4. Accept Challenges: Accepting challenges and learning from them is a great way to grow as a person. It is important to be open to new experiences and to learn from them.

5. Celebrate Success: Celebrating success is a great way to stay motivated and continue to strive towards success. It is important to take time to recognize and reward yourself for achievements.

Reflection on The High 5 Habit is a great way to become aware of your behaviors and attitude and to improve upon them. It is important to reflect on these five habits to become a better person.

Moving Forward with The High 5 Habit

The High 5 Habit is a unique approach to personal and professional growth that focuses on building five important habits into your daily routine.

The five habits are: show up, stay focused, get organized, keep learning and stay connected.

Showing up is more than just being physically present. It is about being present with a positive attitude and having the willingness to take on challenges. Showing up is about being present with a purpose and showing initiative.

Staying focused is about being mindful of your goals and staying on track. It is about being intentional and making sure that you are working towards achieving those goals and objectives. Staying focused means not getting distracted by other tasks or conversations and staying on track with the task at hand.

Getting organized is about having a plan and a system in place. It is about having a system that helps you keep track of tasks, manage your time and resources, and get things done. Getting organized helps to ensure that tasks are completed efficiently and on time.

Keep learning is about constantly challenging yourself and developing new skills. It is about taking the time to learn new skills and technologies that can help you to become more productive and successful in your career.

Keeping learning is also about having a growth mindset and being open to new ideas and perspectives.

Staying connected is about building relationships and networking with others. It is about staying in contact with colleagues, mentors, and friends and staying up to date with the latest trends in your industry. Staying connected is also about being a part of the conversation and being involved in the community.

The High 5 Habit is a great way to improve your personal and professional life. It helps to ensure that you are staying organized, staying focused, and staying connected. It also encourages you to learn new skills and stay up to date on industry trends. By implementing the High 5 Habit, you can ensure that you are always working towards your goals and objectives.

Tips for Maintaining and Improving the High 5 Habit

The High 5 Habit is the practice of regularly taking five minutes to focus on something that brings joy, peace, and balance to your life.

Elevate Your Life

It can be anything that brings you a sense of connection and peace, such as reading a book, meditating, listening to music, going for a walk, or simply taking a few moments to appreciate nature.

Here are some tips for maintaining and improving the High 5 Habit:

1. Make it a routine: Set a specific time each day that you dedicate to your High 5. It could be the same time each day or it could vary depending on your schedule. Make sure to stick to your routine and make it a priority.

2. Choose an activity: Choose an activity that you enjoy and that relaxes you. This could be anything from reading, listening to music, doing yoga, or simply taking a few moments to appreciate nature.

3. Take it outside: If possible, take your High 5 outside. Fresh air and nature can help to relax and energize you.

4. Get creative: Don't be afraid to get creative with your High 5. Try something new or add a new twist to an existing activity.

Elevate Your Life

5. Make it social: Invite a friend or family member to join you on your High 5. This can be a great way to cultivate your connection with others and boost your mood.

By following these tips, you can maintain and improve the High 5 Habit. It's important to remember that the High 5 Habit is about taking regular moments to connect with yourself, so make sure to make it a priority and enjoy the moments.

Final Thoughts and Encouragement

In Elevate Your Life, you have learned about the power of the High 5 Habits and how to use them to make positive changes in your life. You have been given the tools and resources to take ownership of your life and make it better. The key is to take action, practice the High 5 Habits, and be consistent. As you incorporate these habits into your life, you will find that your life is elevated and you can achieve your goals.

Take this knowledge and use it to make your life better. Believe in yourself and be confident that you can make positive changes. Be ready to make mistakes but don't let them define you. Instead, use them as learning experiences and keep improving.

I hope you have found this book to be helpful and inspiring. I wish you all the best on your journey of personal growth.

www.ingramcontent.com/pod-product-compliance
Lightning Source LLC
Chambersburg PA
CBHW071148240526
45465CB00024BA/1916